Types of eruption

D0532810

Surtseyan

Key features

- **Underwater volcano erupting explosively at water's surface**
- **Blasts out ash and larger fragments called cinders**
- **May form new island**

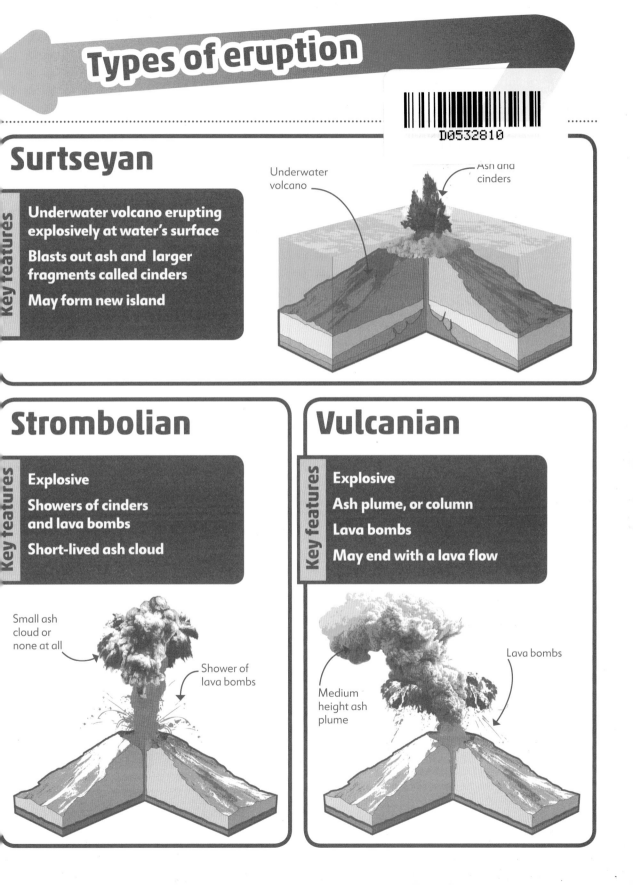

Underwater volcano

Ash and cinders

Strombolian

Key features

- **Explosive**
- **Showers of cinders and lava bombs**
- **Short-lived ash cloud**

Small ash cloud or none at all

Shower of lava bombs

Vulcanian

Key features

- **Explosive**
- **Ash plume, or column**
- **Lava bombs**
- **May end with a lava flow**

Medium height ash plume

Lava bombs

Things to find out:

DK findout!

Volcanoes

Author: Maria Gill
Consultant: Robert Dinwiddie

Schools Library & Museum Service
Unit D
Ropemaker Park
HAILSHAM
East Sussex BN27 3GU
Tel: 01323 466380

04359622 - ITEM

Penguin Random House

Project editor Sam Priddy
Designer Emma Hobson
Senior editor Jolyon Goddard
Managing editor Laura Gilbert
Managing art editor Diane Peyton Jones
Picture researcher Surya Sarangi
Pre-production producer Dragana Puvacic
Producer Srijana Gurung
Art director Martin Wilson
Publisher Sarah Larter
Publishing director Sophie Mitchell

Educational consultant Jacqueline Harris

First published in Great Britain in 2016 by
Dorling Kindersley Limited
80 Strand, London, WC2R 0RL

Copyright © 2016 Dorling Kindersley Limited
A Penguin Random House Company
10 9 8 7 6 5 4 3 2 1
001–291663–Jul/2016

All rights reserved.
No part of this publication may be reproduced, stored in
or introduced into a retrieval system, or transmitted, in
any form, or by any means (electronic, mechanical,
photocopying, recording, or otherwise), without the
prior written permission of the copyright owner.

A CIP catalogue record for this book
is available from the British Library.
ISBN: 978-0-2412-5024-2

Printed and bound in China

A WORLD OF IDEAS:
SEE ALL THERE IS TO KNOW

www.dk.com

Contents

EAST SUSSEX
SCHOOLS LIBRARY
SERVICE

580140	04359622
Askews & Holts	Feb-2017
550 GIL	£5.99

Maleo

Fly Ranch Geyser

Hand glass

Dacite

Pumice

Basalt

Devil's Tower

The sound of Krakatau's eruption in 1883 was heard 4,800 km (3,000 miles) away.

What is a volcano?

A volcano is an opening in the Earth's surface out of which hot melted rock, called magma, erupts. The opening is often at the top of a mountain. When magma flows out of a volcano it is known as lava. Magma can also be blasted out as clouds of smaller particles, called ash, along with gas given off by the magma.

Volcanic eruption

Magma builds up underground until it erupts through the volcano's vents. Eruptions may go on until the magma chamber is empty.

! WOW!

About **60 volcanoes** erupt in the world **each year.**

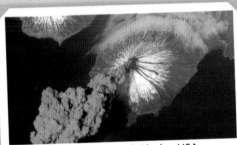

Mount Cleveland, Alaska, USA

Irazú Volcano, Costa Rica

Not all volcanoes look the same. Many are high, snow-capped mountains and others have huge craters, often filled with a lake. Some volcanoes are islands and others are completely under the sea.

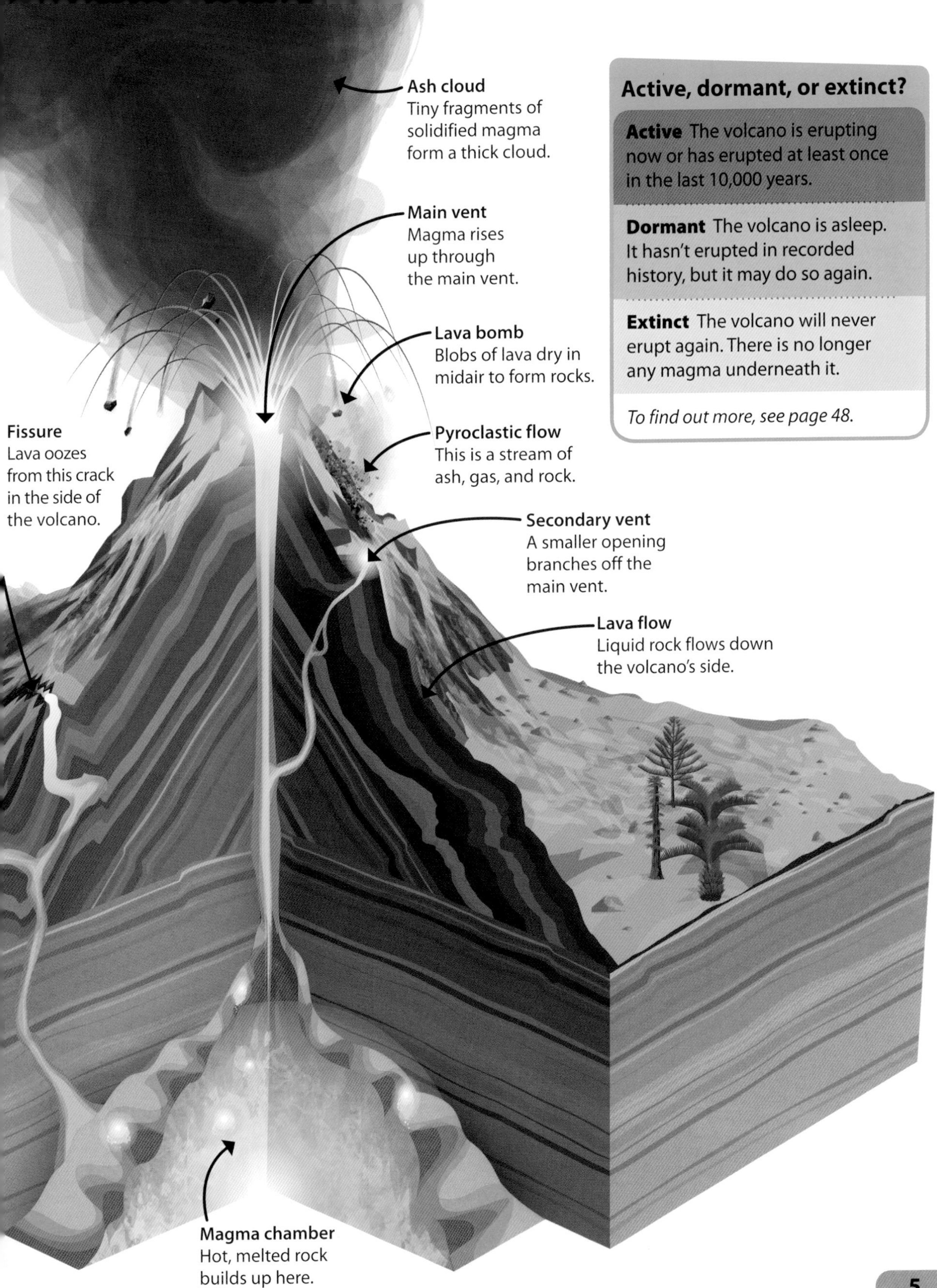

Ash cloud
Tiny fragments of
solidified magma
form a thick cloud.

Main vent
Magma rises
up through
the main vent.

Lava bomb
Blobs of lava dry in
midair to form rocks.

Fissure
Lava oozes
from this crack
in the side of
the volcano.

Pyroclastic flow
This is a stream of
ash, gas, and rock.

Secondary vent
A smaller opening
branches off the
main vent.

Lava flow
Liquid rock flows down
the volcano's side.

Active, dormant, or extinct?

Active The volcano is erupting
now or has erupted at least once
in the last 10,000 years.

Dormant The volcano is asleep.
It hasn't erupted in recorded
history, but it may do so again.

Extinct The volcano will never
erupt again. There is no longer
any magma underneath it.

To find out more, see page 48.

Magma chamber
Hot, melted rock
builds up here.

Inside the Earth

The Earth has several layers. Its outer layer, called the crust, floats on a layer of hot rock called the mantle. This thick layer is split into the semi-solid upper mantle and the solid lower mantle. At the Earth's centre is its metal core, made of an outer liquid layer and inner solid ball. Volcanoes appear when melted rock in the mantle breaks through the Earth's crust.

Cutting through the Earth
The picture below shows you what the Earth would look like if we cut it in half.

Crust
The Earth's rocky outer layer, called the crust, is its thinnest layer. There are two types of crust. Continental crust forms most land, and oceanic crust lies below the seas.

Continental crust

Oceanic crust

Upper mantle
The rock in the upper mantle is hot and can slowly move like a liquid. It contains a lot of the metal magnesium.

Lower mantle
This layer of the Earth is made of hot, solid rock. Like the upper mantle, the rock is rich in the metal magnesium.

Inside knowledge
Nobody has ever drilled down far enough to see the Earth's mantle or core. Scientists have worked out which layers inside the Earth are solid, which are liquid, and what they are made of just by studying the vibrations that travel through the Earth during earthquakes.

Outer core
This part of the Earth's core is made of the metals iron and nickel. It is liquid, unlike the solid inner core.

Inner core
The Earth's centre is a hot, solid ball made of iron and nickel.

Hotspot
In some places in the world, magma plumes break through the Earth's crust, forming new volcanoes. These places are called hotspots.

Mantle plume
Some scientists think that columns of melted rock, or magma, rise up from where the core and mantle meet. These may eventually reach the crust as hotspots.

Feeling the pressure

When you dive to the bottom of a swimming pool, your ears may hurt. This feeling is due to an increase in pressure, caused by the weight of water pressing down on you. Inside the Earth, pressure also increases the deeper you go and drops as you move back up again. When melted rock, or magma, rises inside the Earth, gases in it make bubbles as pressure drops. If this magma pushes out of a volcano, it cools to make lightweight bubbly rocks, such as pumice.

A diver adjusts to the pressure underwater.

REALLY?

The **temperature** at the centre of the **Earth** is about **6,000°C (10,800°F).**

Jigsaw Earth

The Earth's crust, or outer layer, is broken up into huge pieces called tectonic plates. These plates fit together like the pieces of a giant jigsaw puzzle. The plates move incredibly slowly – but very powerfully. Volcanic eruptions and earthquakes are common where the plates meet up.

Mid-Atlantic Ridge

A diver swims between plates that are moving apart.

Ring of Fire
There are many volcanoes on the boundaries that form this ring around the Pacific Ocean.

1
2
3
4
5
6
7
8
9
10
11
12
13

Rift Valley
Africa is slowly splitting apart along this boundary.

San Andreas Fault

The Earth's tectonic plates and their boundaries

Earthquakes are common along the San Andreas Fault in California, USA.

How do the plates move?

Scientists think that slowly moving streams of hot rock deep inside the Earth move tectonic plates. Heat that spreads out from the Earth's core is thought to move the streams.

Hot streams
Below the Earth's crust, streams of hot rock move around in loops. They drag the plates around with them.

THE EARTH'S PLATES

» Key

▨▨▨	Ring of Fire
▨▨▨	Plate boundary
▲	Volcano

1. Philippine Sea plate
2. Australian plate
3. Pacific plate
4. North American plate
5. Cocos plate
6. Caribbean plate
7. Nazca plate
8. South American plate
9. Antarctic plate
10. Scotia plate
11. African plate
12. Eurasian plate
13. Arabian plate
14. Indian plate

Types of boundary

At the boundaries, or edges, of tectonic plates, one of three things can happen. The plates move apart, bump into each other, or slide past each other. Some plates carry continents. Over millions of years, the slow-moving plates have carried the continents across the world. Volcanoes often appear at plate boundaries.

Divergent boundary

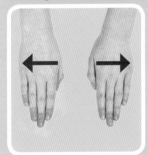

Here, plates move apart. As they do so, volcanoes form, erupting lava and making new crust. On land, these boundaries are known as rifts, such as the Rift Valley in Africa. In the ocean, they are known as ridges, such as the Mid-Atlantic Ridge.

Convergent boundary

At a convergent boundary, plates bump into each other. One plate will slide underneath the other. If a plate below an ocean slides under any other plate, a line of volcanoes will form where they meet, as seen at the boundaries that make the Ring of Fire.

Transform boundary

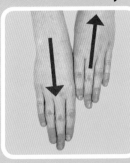

At a transform boundary, two plates slide past each other. They can sometimes become stuck. If they get stuck for too long, pressure builds up until they jerk apart, causing an earthquake. The San Andreas fault in the USA is a transform boundary.

Volcano varieties

When you think of a volcano, you probably imagine a cone with steep sides, spraying out a fountain of red-hot lava or belching thick clouds of ash. However, there are several kinds of volcano. Some have a huge crater, often filled with a lake. Others have sides that are gentle slopes and ooze, rather than spurt, lava. These are the four main types of volcano, with two examples of each.

! WOW!

The word **"caldera"** is Spanish for **"cauldron"**, or **"cooking pot"**.

Cinder cone

Cinder cones are the smallest and most common type of volcano. They are made of cooled fragments of lava, called cinders. These volcanoes often form on the sides of bigger volcanoes.

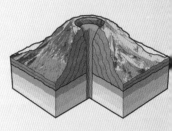

Stratovolcano

The "strato" part of this volcano's name means "layer". This steep-sided cone is built of many layers of lava and ash, caused by many explosive eruptions.

Caldera

Calderas are huge craters. They form when the top part of a stratovolcano collapses. Stratovolcanoes do this when a huge amount of melted rock, or magma, builds up below them and then explodes.

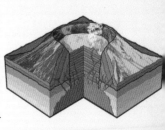

Shield

These giant volcanoes are the shape of an ancient warrior's shield, with gently sloping sides. They are made of layer upon layer of lava that oozed out and cooled to form hard rock.

Parícutin erupted out of a cornfield in 1943, rising to 50 m (164 ft) on the first day. It grew for nine more years, reaching 424 m (1,390 ft).

Parícutin, Mexico

Lava Butte erupted about 7,000 years ago. Astronauts used to train for trips to the Moon in the volcano's crater, as it is similar to the Moon's surface.

Lava Butte, Oregon, USA

Mount Etna has erupted about 190 times since 1226 BCE. It tends to explode very loudly, with long lava flows down its sides.

Mount Etna, Italy

Mount Fuji is a symbol of Japan. This volcano has erupted 16 times since 781 CE, the last explosion happening in 1707.

Mount Fuji, Japan

Mount Aniakchak's caldera formed about 3,400 years ago. There is a lake inside the caldera called Surprise Lake.

Mount Aniakchak, Alaska, USA

Crater Lake is the caldera of a stratovolcano called Mount Mazama, which erupted and then collapsed about 7,700 years ago.

Crater Lake, Oregon, USA

This fountain of lava is erupting from the volcano Kilauea. It is by far the most active of five shield volcanoes that have built the islands of Hawaii.

Kilauea, Hawaii, USA

"Erta Ale" means "smoking mountain" in the local Afar language. There is a lake of boiling lava at the top of this shield volcano.

Erta Ale, Ethiopia

Lots of lava

Molten magma is called lava once it erupts through a gap in the Earth's crust. Scientists classify the four main types of lava by looking at how thick or thin it is, whether it is runny or sticky, what its surface looks like, and where it has erupted.

Pahoehoe lava
Pahoehoe lava is thin, hot lava with a smooth or wrinkled surface. It moves and cools slowly.

Block lava
This lava is very thick when it oozes out of a volcano. It then hardens into large blocks as it cools.

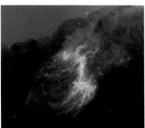

Pillow lava
This lava oozes out of the ocean floor. It forms a glassy crust and expands like a balloon until it cracks.

Aa lava
Aa lava is thick, fast-flowing, and quick to cool. It has a rough and uneven surface.

Lava rocks

After lava is exposed to air and water it cools down to form a type of rock called igneous rock. These rocks look different depending on which minerals the magma absorbs as it passes through the Earth's crust and up out of the volcano.

Pumice is so light that it can float in water!

Basalt
The most common type of rock. It covers most of the ocean floor.

Andesite
A fine-grained rock commonly found on stratovolcanoes, such as Mount Fuji in Japan.

Dacite
A light-coloured rock that often forms mound-like features on volcanoes.

Pumice
A pale-coloured rock full of bubbles of gas that were trapped inside as it formed.

Flowing lava

How far and fast lava flows depends on how much erupts and how thick it is. The type of minerals inside the lava, as well as the type of ground it moves over, also make a difference.

Lava glows bright red when it first erupts. The hotter this aa lava is, the quicker it will move.

As lava cools, it forms a thick black skin and slows down.

WOW!

Lava can cover up to **240 football pitches** in an hour.

Deadliest eruptions

Whole cities can be destroyed when a nearby volcano erupts. If there are warning signs, people have time to leave. If it explodes without warning, thousands of lives may be at risk. Here are the five deadliest eruptions in human history.

5

Nevado del Ruiz, Colombia

23,000 deaths

Main cause: mudflow. On 13 November 1985, a fast-moving stream of hot gas, ash, and rock, called a pyroclastic flow, erupted from Nevado del Ruiz. It melted snow on the volcano's peak and turned into a huge mudflow, or lahar, that destroyed two towns.

4

Mount Pelée, Martinique, in the Caribbean

28,000 deaths

Main cause: pyroclastic flow. In May 1902, a pyroclastic flow from Mount Pelée, travelling at 670 kph (416 mph), destroyed everything in the nearby town of Saint-Pierr

3

Lake Ilopango, El Salvador

30,000 deaths

Main cause: pyroclastic flow. About 1,500 years ago, this volcano, which is now below Lake Ilopango, erupted. A pyroclastic flow from the eruption killed everyone in the nearby Ancient Mayan cities. Most of El Salvador was covered in ash.

2

Krakatau, Indonesia

36,000 deaths

Main causes: landslide and tsunami. In 1883, two-thirds of the island of Krakatau disappeared when its volcano erupted. The violent explosion caused a landslide and a giant wave, or tsunami. The wave spread across the Indian Ocean and destroyed many faraway coastal town and cities.

1

Mount Tambora, Indonesia

90,000 deaths

Main causes: pyroclastic flow and starvation. In 1815, Mount Tambora erupted. A pyroclastic flow killed about 12,000 people near the volcano. Many more died later of starvation because their crops and animals had been destroyed. The massive cloud of ash released by the volcano dimmed sunlight and lowered temperatures across the world.

Blowing its top

Mount St. Helens is a large volcano in the Cascade Range of mountains in northwestern USA. It used to have a cone-shaped peak, but on the morning of 18 May 1980 the volcano's top and north side blew off in an explosive eruption.

! WOW!

The explosion was heard **320 km (200 miles)** away.

» **Date:** 18 May 1980

» **Height:** 2,549 m (8,363 ft)

Devastation

The massive blast of hot gases, rocks, and ash was followed by the largest landslide in recorded history. More than 10 million trees were flattened by the blast, and 57 people, thousands of large animals, and millions of small ones were killed. Plants began to grow back after a few months and birds soon began to return to the area.

Mount St. Helens erupting in 1980

Staying safe

People who live near an active or dormant volcano must always be prepared in case it erupts. They need to make sure they know the signs of an eruption, what they should do, and what items to keep in an emergency survival kit. They need a plan to stay safe until emergency services reach them or advise them what to do next.

Signs of an eruption

Explosion

Can you see smoke or ash coming out of the volcano or volcanic lake? Did you hear an explosion?

Bad smell

Can you smell sulphur? It smells a bit like rotten eggs. If so, wear a gas mask or face mask and goggles.

Shaky ground

Can you feel the ground shaking? If you are outdoors, find shelter as soon as you can.

Survival kit

Electricity and gas may be cut off in the event of a volcanic eruption. You will therefore need a survival kit with the items shown here. Check it regularly to make sure all the items are in working order and up to date. Try to keep all of it in one large bag or box.

Radio

Batteries

BBQ or camping stove

Spare clothes

Blankets

Goggles

Toiletries

Torch

First aid kit

Water

Tinned food

Masks

Emergency plan

If you live near a volcano, your family should have a plan of what to do in case of an eruption. It should include knowing where to meet and where your survival kit is stored. It is a good idea if someone in your family learns basic first aid, too, in case of injuries. The plan should also cover the items described below.

1

Listen to the radio

Make sure you listen to a local radio station for the latest updates about the volcano and advice on what to do.

2

Seek shelter if outside

It will be safer inside a building than outside it. Make sure all the windows and doors are kept closed.

3

Bring pets indoors

Bring any pets you have indoors. They may sense that something is wrong and need calming.

4

Check your family is okay

Make sure your family is safe. You may need to carry out first aid for health problems, such as injuries.

5

Protect yourself against ash

If you come into contact with falling ash, make sure you wear a gas mask or a face mask and goggles.

Wear protective gear if you must go outside.

Always be prepared!

Hazard warning!

Volcanoes cause many hazards before, during, and after eruptions. Most only affect you if you live near one. However, tsunamis and harmful ash can travel thousands of kilometres. Scientists study volcanoes so they can spot the hazard signs and save lives.

Mudflows

Mudflows, also called lahars, are a mix of volcanic ash, rocks, and water that sweep down a volcano after heavy rainfall. Anyone caught in the path of a mudflow could drown or be crushed under the huge volume of material. Mudflows can also destroy buildings and flatten trees in their way.

AVALANCHE

A rockfall or avalanche occurs when heavy rainfall or earthquakes cause unstable debris, such as rocks, snow, or ice, to fall down a steep volcano. Like a mudflow, it will destroy everything in its path.

Ash fall

After a volcano erupts, ash, which is made from billions of tiny pieces of volcanic rock, falls from the sky. Even light amounts of falling volcanic ash can irritate eyes and lungs, prevent planes flying, damage homes, destroy crops, and make water unclean. When Mount Vesuvius erupted in 79 CE, an enormous amount of ash fell on the nearby city of Pompeii. It lay undiscovered for 1,500 years.

TSUNAMIS

Sometimes, underwater earthquakes and volcanic eruptions cause giant sea waves called tsunamis. They can travel great distances and flood coastlines and islands with terrific force, destroying buildings and drowning people and animals.

Pyroclastic flows

After an eruption, deadly clouds of hot gas, ash, and rock particles, called pyroclastic flows, can travel at speeds more than 500 kph (310 mph) along the ground. They can reach temperatures as high as 700°C (1,300°F) and cause fires. A deadly pyroclastic flow happened in 2010 when Mount Merapi, on the Indonesian island of Java, erupted and the flow killed over 300 people.

EARTHQUAKES

Movement of magma underneath a volcano can cause two types of volcanic earthquake. Volcanic tremors warn that a volcano eruption will happen soon. Volcano-tectonic earthquakes cause the ground to change shape or crack, and they can cause landslides down a volcano.

Electrical storms

Ash clouds can trigger powerful electrical charges that produce lightning. Lightning can start fires, cause electrical surges that damage electrical products, and interfere with radio communications.

VULCAN
Roman God of Fire and Crafts

Long ago, the people who lived on the volcanic island of Vulcano, now part of Italy, believed eruptions happened when Vulcan used fire to make weapons. The word "volcano" comes from his name.

PELE
Hawaiian Goddess of Fire

This goddess had an explosive personality. When she used her magic stick to dig, she caused volcanic eruptions. Golden glass threads, which sometimes form from lava, were once believed to be Pele's hair.

Myths and legends

Ancient people did not understand why volcanoes erupted. They thought the cause was due to the anger or actions of their gods or other mysterious supernatural beings. So they made up stories to explain the reasons. These were passed down to us as myths and legends.

SURTR
Viking Fire Giant

The Vikings believed that Surtr would lead the giants against the gods in the final battle on Earth. Before dying, Surtr would sweep his flaming sword across the world, burning everything.

FUCHI
Japanese Goddess of the Hearth

Japan's highest mountain, the volcano Mount Fuji, is named after Fuchi. The ancient people of Japan believed Fuchi lived in the hearth, which is the fireplace used for cooking and heating homes.

Did Atlantis exist?

The Ancient Greeks had a legend about an island called Atlantis. It told that the people who lived there were wicked. They angered the gods, who destroyed the island with fire and earthquakes, until it sank below the sea. Some people now believe this story may be linked to the Greek island of Santorini. About 3,400 years ago, a massive volcanic eruption devastated Santorini. Part of the island fell into the sea, and many people on nearby islands may have died as a result of tsunamis.

Underwater city

Modern-day Santorini

Roman eruption

In 79CE, the volcano Mount Vesuvius, overlooking the Bay of Naples in present-day Italy, suddenly erupted. Pliny the Elder, head of the Roman navy, saw the explosion from a nearby coastal town called Misenum. He sailed his fleet of ships across the bay towards the towns of Pompeii and Herculaneum in an effort to rescue people...

Pliny was forced to abandon his ships at Stabiae, a port 16 km (10 miles) from Vesuvius. The town was being pelted by pumice stones as big as tennis balls.

It's as dark as night!

Pliny waded through the pumice, using torchlight to find shelter. Ash blocked the light from the Sun.

How can he sleep?

Hoping to sail away later, Pliny dined and then had a nap! He tied a pillow to his head to protect himself from falling stones.

When he awoke, Pliny stood up and then collapsed in the arms of two slaves. Volcanic fumes had poisoned him.

In the night, a fast-moving stream of hot gas, ash, and rock, called a pyroclastic flow, raced down the volcano's slopes, scorching and burying everything in its path.

Travelling at 100 kph (60 mph)!

Meanwhile, back in Misenum, Pliny the Elder's 17-year-old nephew, known as Pliny the Younger, recorded everything he saw across the bay.

Pompeii and Herculaneum were forgotten about for many centuries until workman discovered the remains of buildings and people buried under thick ash.

Today, the ruins of Pompeii and Herculaneum attract millions of visitors each year. The homes, temples, workplaces, and other buildings offer us a fascinating look into how people lived in Ancient Roman times.

Mystery of the lake

On 21 August 1986, about 1,800 people living in villages around Lake Nyos, in a volcanic region of Cameroon, died mysteriously in the night. At first, no one knew what had caused this terrible and very unusual event. Scientists were called in to investigate. They soon turned their attention to Lake Nyos...

The next day

The few villagers who survived the night woke up to find that most of their relatives and friends had died. The survivors were also covered in strange sores and blisters. Thousands of cattle, owned by the people in the villages, had died in the night, too.

Studying the lake
Scientists study the water in Lake Nyos to try to figure out what caused the disaster.

LAKE NYOS

Location:
Cameroon, West Africa

The verdict

The scientists discovered that melted rock, or magma, under the volcanic lake releases harmful gas into the water at the bottom of the lake. The gas had built up until a huge cloud of it bubbled out of the lake. Heavier than air, the cold gas flowed rapidly down nearby valleys. It stopped the villagers from breathing and caused sores and blisters.

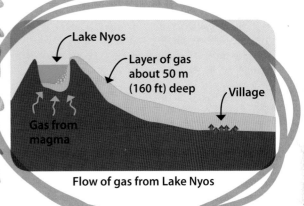

Lake Nyos

Layer of gas about 50 m (160 ft) deep

Village

Gas from magma

Flow of gas from Lake Nyos

The solution

To prevent the disaster from happening again, big pipes have been put in the lake to remove the dangerous gas. Water from the bottom of the lake, where the gas builds up, is pumped to the lake's surface. There, the gas bubbles out in harmless amounts. Other similar lakes now have had the gas in their depths removed in this way, too.

Pipes release gas

Removing the gas

Getting supplies to the disaster site
Planes bring emergency supplies to the villagers who survived the disaster.

Icelandic ash

In 2010, a volcano in Iceland called Eyjafjallajökull belched thousands of tonnes of ash into the sky. The ash rose to a great height, before spreading across a huge area, including most of Europe. Thousands of aeroplane flights were cancelled, with many companies losing millions of pounds.

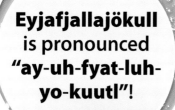

! WOW!

Eyjafjallajökull is pronounced "ay-uh-fyat-luh-yo-kuutl"!

Rising plume

When magma rose up Eyjafjallajökull's vent and reached its summit it mixed with the snow and ice covering the volcano. This mixture made the eruption very explosive. It produced thick clouds of ash that rose in a plume, or column, up to 9 km (6 miles) high.

View from space
This picture was taken three days after Eyjafjallajökull first began to erupt ash. The ash plume can be seen rising high above the snowy volcano.

Flights cancelled
Ash particles can get inside plane engines and stop them from working. In the week after the volcano began to erupt, 20 countries closed their airspace and 95,000 flights were cancelled.

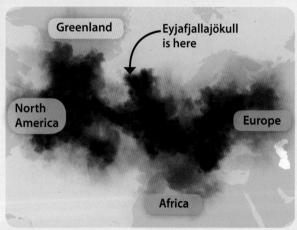

Greenland

Eyjafjallajökull is here

North America

Europe

Africa

Area of ash cloud
Winds blew the ash cloud over most of mainland Europe. Part of the cloud then drifted across the Atlantic Ocean towards North America.

Flood basalts

A flood basalt is an area covered in a type of lava called basalt. These areas formed millions of years ago, when lava poured out of cracks in the ground over thousands of years. The "floods" of lava cooled and hardened to cover huge areas, some as big as large countries in today's world.

! WOW!

There are also **flood basalts** on the **Moon** and the planet **Venus!**

Giant's Causeway, Northern Ireland

Giant steps

Basalt lava sometimes dries to form columns of rocks with a six-sided, or hexagonal, shape. The Giant's Causeway on the coast of Northern Ireland has about 40,000 of these columns. It is part of a flood basalt called the North Atlantic Igneous Province. Legend has it that the giant Finn McCool built the causeway so he could cross the sea to fight a Scottish giant.

How the causeway was formed

About 50 to 60 million years ago, huge amounts of basalt lava erupted out of cracks in the ground. In some areas, it broke up into columns as it cooled.

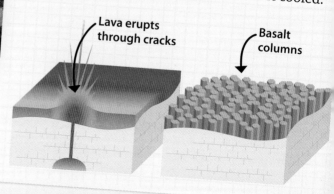

Lava erupts through cracks

Basalt columns

Layers of lava

A huge hilly area of central India, called the Deccan Traps, is covered in dried basalt lava up to 2 km (1.2 miles) thick. The lava came from many great volcanic eruptions that began about 66 million years ago. Layer upon layer of lava built up over thousands of years of eruptions. The word "traps" comes from the Swedish word for "stairway", as the basalt hillsides look like they have steps in them.

Death of the dinosaurs

Some scientists think that the volcanic eruptions that made the Deccan Traps helped to cause the extinction of the dinosaurs. Dust and gases, released along with lava, would have dimmed sunlight and poisoned the air, killing off many types of animal across the world.

Volcanic eruptions may have helped to wipe out the dinosaurs.

Deccan Traps, India

Tremendous traps

The Siberian Traps in Russia cover an area larger than Mexico. Volcanic eruptions began in the region about 250 million years ago. Lava gushed out of many huge cracks in the ground, thousands of kilometres apart. The eruptions continued for a million years. The ash released by the eruptions dimmed sunlight so much that global temperatures dropped and the Earth entered a mini ice age.

The Siberian Traps are the largest flood basalt in the world!

Siberian Traps, Russia

Whiffy wonders

When water and magma meet underground, they create interesting natural features called mud pots, geysers, and fumaroles. Mud pots bubble and splutter, geysers spurt jets of boiling water, and fumaroles release hissing steam and gases. And they are all rather smelly!

! WOW!

Steamboat Geyser in the USA spurts water up to **91 m (300 ft)** high.

Bubbling...

In some places, gases released by magma mix with water in the ground to make powerful chemicals that can melt rock. What you end up with is boiling, gloopy clay, bubbling up onto the Earth's surface in pools called mud pots.

Mud sometimes splats out over the edge of the pool.

FACT FILE

» **Name:** Hverir Mud Pots

» **Location:** Iceland

» **Pong power:** 8

... spurting...

In 1964, a team of oil-drilling engineers forgot to close a hole in the ground. Soon, a geyser appeared, spurting superhot water and forming these colourful cones.

The cones are coated in colourful, tiny life-forms called algae.

Water spurts nonstop.

FACT FILE

» **Name:** Fly Ranch Geyser

» **Location:** USA

» **Pong power:** 5

... and hissing!

When magma mixes with underground water, it makes stinky steam. The steam hisses as it escapes from the ground, through cracks or cones called fumaroles.

The steam smells like rotten eggs!

FACT FILE

» **Name:** Dallol Fumaroles

» **Location:** Ethiopia

» **Pong power:** 10

Caves

Wherever there are volcanoes, there are caves, too. Many of these caves are empty tunnels, or tubes, through which hot lava once flowed. Other caves contain huge crystals made of minerals from magma. There are also small caves, in volcanic regions, that were carved out by people long ago.

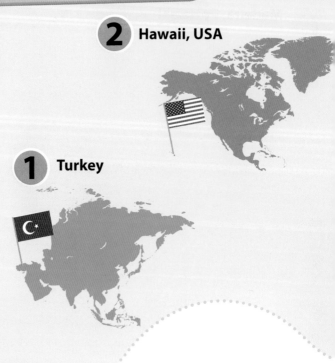

2 Hawaii, USA

1 Turkey

A Long tunnels

The caves and tunnels on this island in the Atlantic Ocean were made after a volcanic eruption hundreds of thousands of years ago.

Colossal crystals

When miners drained this cave in North America, they found 11 m- (36 ft-) long crystals, made from minerals in magma-heated water.

B

3 Madeira, Portugal

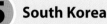
5 South Korea

4 Mexico

C

Underwater grotto

Lava flowing into the sea can make underwater caves. The one shown here lies off an island in the Pacific Ocean.

E Cave houses

Millions of years ago, volcanoes erupted in this region, where Europe meets Asia. Wind and rain eroded the layers of volcanic rock, creating some strangely shaped hills. Much later, ancient people carved out cave homes in the hillsides.

D

Spiky space

This amazing lava cave in East Asia contains dangling stalactites, upright stalagmites, stone pillars, and rocks that look like coral.

A world without volcanoes...

What would a world without volcanoes be like? The answer is truly mind-blowing! As well as spewing out burning-hot lava, volcanoes have played a key role in building the world we live in.

Feeling thirsty? You can thank volcanoes for refreshing drinks.

Water

Water is essential to life on Earth, and volcanoes helped supply it! When volcanoes first erupted, water in the gases they released turned to liquid, and this was added to the Earth's oceans.

Natural wonders

As you flick through your holiday snaps, did you know some of those beautiful landmarks were created by volcanoes? You can thank volcanoes for many of the deep canyons, massive mountains, and spectacular waterfalls on this planet.

Devil's Tower in the US state of Wyoming was formed by an ancient volcano.

Hawaii

Canary Islands

Both of these island chains were formed by volcanic eruptions.

Volcanic islands

As you walk along a sandy beach, it's worth remembering that a volcano may have created the island you are standing on. When an underwater volcano erupts, the lava may eventually break the surface of the water, forming an island.

Soil

Soil may not sound exciting, but we need good soil to grow the fruit and vegetables we eat. Volcanic ash is rich in minerals that are great for growing plants.

Farming near volcanoes can be dangerous, but without volcanoes some communities wouldn't be able to grow the crops they need to survive.

Diamonds

Diamonds are the most precious jewels on the planet, but we wouldn't ever see them if not for volcanoes. Diamonds form at extreme temperatures and pressure deep within the Earth. Volcanoes bring them up to the surface.

At some point, this diamond came up through the Earth's surface in a volcano.

Climate change

Truly catastrophic eruptions can cause the global temperature to drop by a few degrees. This is because the ash and gas propelled into the atmosphere prevent some of the Sun's heat from reaching the ground.

A few degrees can be the difference between frozen ice cream and melted ice cream!

Supermagnets

Believe it or not, volcanoes helped make smartphones. When molten iron cools, it hardens into supermagnets a thousand times stronger than normal magnets. They are used to make hi-tech products.

Wind turbines use supermagnets to help produce electricity.

Hot habitats

Volcanoes seem to be unlikely places for animals to live. However, many animals spend time or make their homes in hot volcanic regions. Some like the warmth of hot springs or volcanic ash. Others feed on the tiny life-forms that have found a way to survive in the harsh conditions of volcanic lakes. Here are four animals that find volcanoes very useful.

Bathing beauties

Japanese macaques keep themselves warm in the chilly winter months by relaxing and grooming each other in the hot springs of Japan's volcanic hills. The thick fur of these monkeys helps them cope with the hot water.

Pretty in pink

These flamingos have rosy pink feathers because of what they eat. They feed on algae, tiny life-forms related to seaweed, in a volcanic lake called Lake Natron, in Africa. The algae are able to survive in the hot, harsh lake. After the flamingos have eaten, a chemical in the algae turns their feathers pink.

Warm nest

Female maleo birds lay 8–12 large eggs each year. They dig a burrow and bury their eggs up to 1.5 m (5 ft) deep in warm volcanic ash or sand, which has a temperature of about 35°C (95°F). The maleo chicks hatch underground and then dig themselves out. Within a few hours, the little birds can fly and look after themselves without any help.

The maleo lets volcanic soil warm its eggs.

Clever birds

Most birds sit on their eggs, so that the developing chicks inside keep warm. The maleo, which lives in Indonesia, has found a way to avoid this chore. This animal is part of a group of birds called megapodes, or mound builders. It buries its eggs in warm volcanic ash or sand and then wanders off – never to return!

Living on lava

Lava lizards are found on the volcanic Galápagos Islands, which lie off the coast of South America. These small reptiles spend their days scurrying over bare dried lava, looking for tasty insects to gobble up. To impress females, male lava lizards do push-ups!

Volcanic lightning

Flashes of lightning during thunderstorms, or electrical storms, are a familiar sight. Lightning can also happen during volcanic eruptions. Scientists do not fully understand what causes volcanic lightning. They think it is due to tiny particles in the ash cloud rubbing together and becoming electrically charged.

Colliding particles
An electrostatic charge is created by colliding ash particles.

Lightning
The build-up of electrostatic charge turns into lightning.

Flash with ash

As particles of ash in a volcanic eruption rub together they create an electrostatic charge. The charge builds up until it eventually turns into a flow of electricity, or an electric current. This current explodes the air around it, creating a flash of lightning. The noise of this explosion is thunder.

Dirty thunderstorm

Mount Etna, on the island of Sicily, Italy, erupted in late 2015 with a dazzling display of lava, ash, and lightning. The ash cloud climbed 3 km (1.9 miles). Volcanologists call eruptions with lightning "dirty thunderstorms".

WOW!

Mount St. Helens in the USA produced **a bolt of lightning every second** when it erupted in 1980.

WOW!

Volcanologists have used **robots** to try to reach areas that are **too dangerous** for humans.

The suit's silver colour reflects heat and helps to keep the volcanologist cool.

Meet the expert

We put some questions to volcanologist Dr Gill Jolly, who does one of the most dangerous jobs on Earth.

Q: We know your job is something to do with volcanoes, but what do you actually do?

A: I study volcanoes as part of a team. When monitoring an active volcano, we collect samples of rocks, ash, and lava and take measurements. Back at the observatory, we analyse the samples.

Q: It sounds dangerous – how do you keep safe when you work on a volcano?

A: We wear hard hats to protect us from flying rocks, and gas masks to protect us from poisonous gases. We sometimes wear fireproof overalls, like fighter pilots, to protect us from burns.

Q: What tools do you use when you study volcanoes?

A: I use a hammer and hand glass so I can look at rocks and understand what they are. I also take a notebook and camera to make observations. Sometimes, we use satellites to monitor volcanoes. It means we can safely read the information from our computer instead of sticking our heads down a volcanic vent!

Q: What is the best bit about your job?

A: Volcanology is an exciting subject as you're looking at a volcano in real time. You can see a mountain being built or destroyed in front of your eyes!

Q: What is the worst bit about your job?

A: If we have to tell people to evacuate their homes, they tend to see us as being the people who are disrupting their lives.

Q: What was your most exciting experience?

A: When a volcano erupted on the island of Montserrat, in the Caribbean, we flew around it and took photographs and videos. We learned new information about that type of volcanic explosion, as we were able to record the whole eruption sequence.

Montserrat

Q: How good are volcanologists at telling when a volcano is going to erupt?

A: We've had a pretty good success rate. For example, in 2010 in Indonesia, a volcanologist saw the signs and raised an alert. Thousands were evacuated and saved from the eruption.

Tools of the trade

What do volcanologists wear and take with them when they hike up erupting volcanoes, walk over fiery volcanic rocks, or peer into bubbling lakes of lava? Find out about the equipment they need when working in the danger zone.

A bubble inside the tiltmeter moves if the ground tilts – like a builder's spirit level.

Photographs of a volcano taken from all angles can be used to make a 3D model of it.

Notebook
Volcanologists make notes when they visit volcanoes. They record where their samples are taken from and make sketches of rock layers and the landscape.

Cameras
Taking photographs and videos of volcanic activity lets volcanologists study eruptions closely. They also use photographs to work out the height of eruptions.

Tiltmeter
This instrument measures the tilt, or slope, of the ground. On the slopes of a volcano, a small change in the tilt could mean that it is about to erupt.

Webcam
This video camera can be set up near a volcano and left to film its activity.

In action
Volcanologists like to get where the action is. They take photographs of eruptions, record vibrations in the ground, and collect samples of red-hot lava or falling ash.

Seismometer
This instrument picks up vibrations in the ground caused by volcanic activity.

Preparing the seismometer

Heat suit

This silver-coloured heat suit contains the metal aluminium and can withstand temperatures as high as 1,650°C (3,000°F)!

Helmet
The head is protected from flying rocks by a tough helmet.

Gas mask
Inside the helmet, a gas mask stops the volcanologist from breathing in poisonous gases.

Hand glass

This tool contains a magnifying glass, which makes things appear much bigger. Volcanologists use it to see the fine details in volcanic rocks.

Looking at lava rocks
Lava rocks may contain crystals or fragments of other rocks.

Breathing tanks strapped on back
Tanks supply cool fresh air when the air outside is too hot or poisonous to breathe in.

Gloves
Tough gloves protect the hands from hot rocks and lava.

Heavy boots
Thick leather boots stop the feet from getting burned when walking in hot volcanic areas.

Hammer and drill

Volcanologists often use a hammer or drill to break off rock samples. These can then be taken away and analysed in a lab.

dangerous job

Sizzling heat, shaky ground, and deafening noises are just a few of the risks volcanologists face. When visiting a volcano, they must stay safe and be on the lookout for dangers such as flying rocks and lava flows.

Lava
Volcanologists extract red-hot lava to study back in their lab.

Samples
The lava samples are cooled in water.

Collecting lava samples

⚠ Supervolcanoes

The volcanoes with the biggest eruptions are called supervolcanoes. Their explosions are much greater than anything we've seen in the past 500 years. The ash they throw out can block sunlight and cool the Earth. There are only a few supervolcanoes in the world. They are all dormant (asleep), but scientists are watching them closely in case any show signs of waking up!

Lake Toba, Sumatra

The eruption here 74,000 years ago was the biggest volcanic eruption in the last 2.5 million years. Ash from the blast fell on areas thousands of kilometres away. Supervolcanoes, like Toba, are caldera volcanoes. They have a huge crater, called a caldera.

Supervolcano checklist

Blasts out at least 1,000 cubic kilometres (240 cubic miles) of rock and magma, enough to cover a country the size of Egypt in 1 m (3.3 ft) of ash or rock ✔

Has had at least one previous massive eruption ✔

Could have another massive eruption in the future ✔

Previous eruptions changed the landscape and climate of the world ✔

FACT FILE

» **Name:** Toba Caldera

» **Status:** Dormant

» **Last super-eruption:** 74,000 years ago

» **Size of blast:** 2,800 cubic kilometres (672 cubic miles)

» **Location:** Northern Sumatra, Indonesia

Volcanic island in lake

A lake fills the caldera.

Yellowstone Park, USA

A massive amount of magma lies below Yellowstone Park. Three major eruptions have reshaped this region in the past, each leaving a huge caldera, or crater. Millions of tourists visit the park each year to see the geysers and hot springs.

Spurting geyser

FACT FILE

» **Name:** Yellowstone Caldera

» **Status:** Dormant

» **Last super-eruption:** 640,000 years ago

» **Size of blast:** 1,000 cubic kilometres (240 cubic miles)

» **Location:** Yellowstone Park, Wyoming, USA

Colourful hot spring

Ash fall from Yellowstone
The last eruption in Yellowstone, 640,000 years ago, threw out so much ash that it covered about half the area of present-day USA.

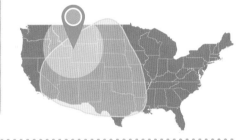

Lake Taupo, New Zealand

When the supervolcano under Lake Taupo erupted 26,500 years ago, it covered most of New Zealand in ash and cooled the southern hemisphere. Since then, it has had many more eruptions, but smaller.

Magma lies below lake.

Steam rises from a tiny crater.

FACT FILE

» **Name:** Taupo Caldera

» **Status:** Dormant

» **Last super-eruption:** 26,500 years ago

» **Size of blast:** 1,170 cubic kilometres (281 cubic miles)

» **Location:** North Island, New Zealand

The life of a volcano

There are thousands of volcanoes dotted around the world, all at different stages in their lives. Some are young, rising from the ground and erupting in recent times. Many seem to be asleep, or dormant, threatening to wake up one day. Others are long dead, or extinct.

! WOW!

There are about **500** active volcanoes on land and many more **under the sea!**

ACTIVE

An active volcano is a volcano that has erupted at least once in the last 10,000 years. It may be erupting now or be ready to erupt at any time.

Active magma chamber

DORMANT

A dormant volcano has not erupted for a few thousand years. It is still very dangerous because it might wake up from its sleep and erupt again.

Magma chamber slowly filling

EXTINCT

An extinct volcano has not erupted for at least 10,000 years. It is not likely to erupt again because there is no longer a supply of magma below it.

Empty magma chamber

Perched on a volcanic plug

This church, called Saint-Michel d'Aiguilhe, was built on top of a plug of dried lava, which blocked the vent of an extinct volcano in central France. You have to walk up 268 steps to visit the church, which is over 1,000 years old.

EXTINCT

Sinking islands

When some undersea volcanoes erupt, they release enough lava or ash to form a new island. The island may stay there permanently or disappear within months, washed away by the sea. Other volcanic islands disappear more gradually, sinking slowly over thousands of years.

The short-lived island caused a few countries to fall out.

FACT FILE

» **Name:** Graham Island, Ferdinandea, or Julia!

» **Status:** Active

» **Last eruption:** 1863

» **Location:** Between Sicily (now part of Italy) and the coast of Africa, in the Mediterranean Sea

Claiming the island

Where's my island gone?

In 1831, a new volcanic island rose out of the Mediterranean Sea near Sicily. A month later, a British sailor planted a Union Jack flag in its cooling lava, claiming it for the UK. He named it Graham Island. Soon after, the Sicilians claimed it for themselves, renaming it Ferdinandea. Then, the French decided it was theirs, calling it Julia. While these countries quarrelled over the island, it sank back into the sea!

Changing flags
In its short life, Graham Island was renamed twice and claimed by the British, Sicilians, and French. The island briefly reappeared in 1863.

Disappearing beauty

Bora Bora is one of the most beautiful islands in the world. It formed about 4 million years ago from the eruption of an underwater volcano. A ring-shaped coral island, called an atoll, grew around it (see below). The now-extinct volcano is sinking very slowly. One day, the island will disappear below the sea, leaving the atoll, with a shallow lake, called a lagoon, inside it.

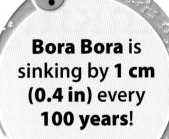

! WOW!

Bora Bora is sinking by 1 cm (0.4 in) every 100 years!

FACT FILE

» **Name:** Bora Bora

» **Status:** Extinct

» **Last eruption:** Unknown

» **Location:** Society Islands, French Polynesia, in the South Pacific Ocean

Plants grow on top of the coral reef.

How an atoll forms

An atoll forms when a coral reef grows around a new volcanic island in the ocean. The reef builds up from the skeletons of corals, which are tiny animals. Eventually it pokes above the sea, and the island sinks, leaving an atoll with a lagoon in the middle.

New volcano
A coral reef begins to grow around the underwater slopes of a new volcanic island.

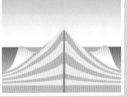

Sinking island
After the volcano stops erupting, it begins to sink, but the coral reef keeps growing.

Atoll and lagoon
The volcano gradually sinks out of sight, leaving an atoll and a shallow lagoon.

New islands

Volcanoes under the sea get bigger each time they erupt. Eventually, their peaks may rise out of the water as new islands. For thousands of years a volcano has been growing near the island of Hunga Tonga in the Pacific Ocean. It suddenly erupted in 2009, spewing huge clouds of smoke and ash high into the air. It erupted again between late 2014 and early 2015 and created a brand-new island.

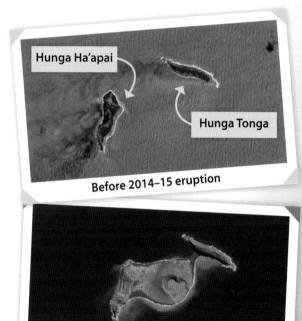

Hunga Ha'apai

Hunga Tonga

Before 2014–15 eruption

After 2014–15 eruption

Before the 2014–15 eruption of the volcano near Hunga Tonga, there were two little volcanic islands poking out of the ocean. When the volcano stopped erupting in 2015, a new area of land had risen out of the sea between the two islands.

A column of **ash** blasted out of the sea and rose to **9 km (6 miles)** in the sky.

Surtsey, Iceland

In 1963, fishermen aboard a boat near Iceland noticed smoke coming out of the sea. A day later, a small island had appeared. The island grew in size with further eruptions, which ended in 1967. It was named Surtsey. However, the wind and waves have since worn away half the island. Scientists think Surtsey might disappear below sea level by 2100. In the meantime, many plants and animals, including these birds, have made the island their home.

Kittiwake

Great black-backed gull

Black guillemot

Northern fulmar

Deep-sea vents

A lot of volcanic activity takes place under the ocean floor. In the 20th century, scientists discovered hydrothermal vents. These are openings in the ocean floor that spurt out billowing clouds of superhot seawater, rich in a variety of minerals.

Underwater hydrothermal vent
The scientific word "hydrothermal" comes from the Greek words for "water" and "heat".

Cold seawater
Very cold seawater, about 2ºC (36ºF), seeps through cracks in the ocean floor.

Exploring the sea

More is known about the surface of the Moon than the Earth's ocean floor. To help explore the ocean depths, scientists use small underwater vehicles called submersibles, such as DeepSee, shown here. Some hold a very small crew. Others work without a crew.

Living in hot water

In the 1970s, scientists were amazed to find many animals and microscopic life-forms called bacteria surviving in the pitch-black, scalding-hot, mineral-rich waters around hydrothermal vents.

Yeti crab
This furry deep-sea crab was only discovered in 2005. It is blind, lives off bacteria, and grows up to 15 cm (6 in) long.

Black smoker
When a mineral chimney releases dark clouds of hot, mineral-rich water, it is called a "black smoker".

Mineral chimney
Minerals from the hot water settle to form fast-growing chimneys.

Rising hot water
Water, heated by magma to temperatures as high as 400°C (750°F), rises up the hydrothermal vent.

Minerals
Microscopic life-forms called bacteria use these chemicals, spewed out from the vents, as their source of energy.

Magma
Seawater travels far below the ocean floor, where magma heats it. On the way back up, it picks up minerals from rocks it moves through.

Deep ocean scale worm
Just 2.5 cm (1 in) long, this scary-looking worm shoots out its jaws to catch its dinner.

Giant tube worms
These red-tipped worms grow up to 2.4 m (8 ft) long. They feed on bacteria and hide in their tubes if they are threatened.

Volcanoes in space

Volcanoes haven't just shaped the Earth – they've also shaped other planets and their moons in our Solar System. Many of these volcanoes in space have been extinct for millions of years, but some are very much alive. Most of our knowledge about these volcanoes has been collected by spacecraft called probes.

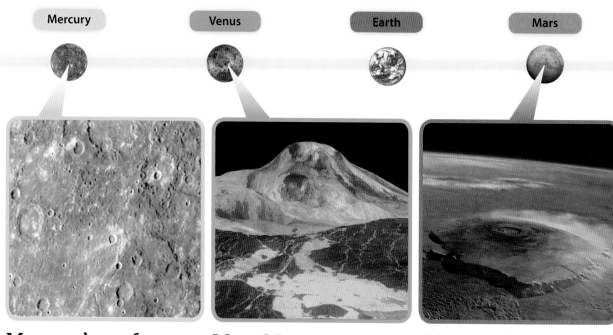

Mercury   Venus   Earth   Mars

Mercury's surface

There are no active volcanoes on Mercury any more. Many craters, however, are found on this planet. They were caused by asteroids and comets hitting Mercury billions of years ago. Lava flows from volcanoes later smoothed the insides of some of these huge craters.

Maat Mons

Venus has more than a thousand volcanoes. The tallest is Maat Mons, which is 8 km (5 miles) high. Thick cloud surrounds the planet, but scientists can use radar to see its surface. They think that some of Venus's volcanoes are still active.

Olympus Mons

Mars has the biggest known volcano in the Solar System. It is called Olympus Mons and is 25 km (15 miles) high. That's almost three times taller than the Earth's Mount Everest! Scientists do not yet know if any of Mars's volcanoes are still active.

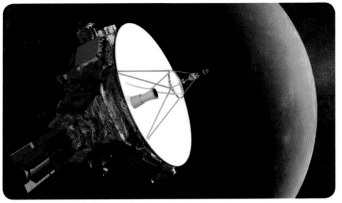

The *New Horizons* probe flew by Jupiter's moon Io in 2007.

Exploring the Solar System

Space probes are robotic spacecraft that are launched from Earth to explore space. They take photographs and gather information, before sending it back to Earth. Some probes are programmed to orbit, or circle around, planets and moons. Others gather information just by flying past, and a few have even made landings. Probes have helped us understand the Solar System and have discovered many volcanoes in space.

Jupiter

Saturn

Uranus

Neptune

Io

Hundreds of active volcanoes are found on Io, one of Jupiter's moons. Some erupt explosively, shooting up columns of gas and dust that rise hundreds of kilometres. Others form huge craters with great lava lakes. There are also lava flows 500 km (300 miles) long.

Enceladus

There are huge geysers on Enceladus, which is one of Saturn's moons. The geysers spurt water and gases from an ocean that lies hidden underneath Enceladus's icy crust. This type of geyser is also called an ice volcano, or cryovolcano.

Triton

Like Enceladus, Neptune's largest moon, Triton, has geysers. They spurt columns of nitrogen and dark dust. The columns can rise 8 km (5 miles) before being blown away by the wind. They also leave long dark streaks on the moon's surface.

Volcano facts and figures

Volcanoes are a fascinating subject. Here are some weird and wonderful facts you might not know about them!

INDONESIA

is the country with the most active volcanoes – **76** have been observed erupting!

There are about 1,550 active volcanoes in the world.

There are about **2,000 volcanologists** in the world today!

74,000 YEARS

since a supervolcano, called Toba, in Indonesia, erupted. It plunged the world into a **10-year-long cold spell**.

20

is the average number of Earth's volcanoes erupting on any day.

300,000,000

is the number of people thought to live within the range of an active volcano.

20,000,000 tonnes

(22,000,000 tons) of the poisonous gas sulphur dioxide were given out by Mount Pinatubo in the Philippines, in 1991. The eruption lowered the world's temperature by 0.5°C (1°F).

60 km (37 miles) is the maximum height that an ash column can reach after an eruption.

Most active volcano

in the world is Kilauea in Hawaii, USA. This volcano has been erupting nonstop since 1983!

Most of this volcano is under the sea.

6,893 m (22,615 ft)

10,204 m (33,476 ft)

75%

is the proportion of Earth's volcanoes that are on the Ring of Fire in the Pacific Ocean.

Highest peak

Ojos del Salado, South America

This volcano's peak is the highest in the air.

Highest from base

Mauna Kea, Hawaii, USA

The base of this volcano is deep in the ocean.

Glossary

Here are the meanings of some words that are useful for you to know when learning all about volcanoes.

active Word used to describe a volcano that is erupting now or has erupted in the last 10,000 years

ash Tiny solid particles formed from lava blasted out of a volcano

atoll Ring-shaped coral island that forms around a slowly sinking volcano

basalt Volcanic rock or lava that is rich in the metals iron and magnesium

BCE Before Common Era, or all the years before year 0

black smoker Volcanic vent on the seafloor that belches out dark clouds of superhot water and minerals

caldera Huge crater that may form after a very large volcanic eruption

CE Common Era, or all the years after year 0

cinder cone Type of volcano mainly made of layers of lava fragments called cinders

continental crust Outer layer of the Earth with land on it

convergent boundary Where tectonic plates are moving towards each other

core Centre of the Earth, made of iron and nickel

A **volcano** forms when **magma** is erupted.

crater Bowl-shaped hole in the top part of a volcano

crust Outer layer of the Earth

cryovolcano Huge geyser seen on distant moons that erupts water and gas rather than molten rock

divergent boundary Where tectonic plates are moving away from each other

dormant Word used to describe a volcano that has not erupted in the past few thousand years but could do so in the future

earthquake Shaking of the Earth's surface caused by shifting tectonic plates or volcanic activity

eruption When lava, ash, rock, or gas shoots or flows out of a volcano

extinct Word used to describe a volcano that will never erupt again

flood basalt Huge area of land covered in thick layers of a type of lava called basalt

fumarole Hole in the ground in a volcanic region from which steam and gas escape

geyser Hot spring that spurts a column of water and steam into the air

hotspot Place where very hot rock inside the Earth rises up as a plume, or column, into the crust and breaks through to form a volcano

hot spring Place in a volcanic region where hot water from underground bubbles up to the Earth's surface

lahar Mudflow of water mixed with volcanic ash and other debris, such as rocks

landslide Sliding of loose soil and rock down a steep slope

lava Hot, melted rock that has come out of a volcano

lava bomb Big blob of lava thrown out during an eruption that cools into rock in midair

magma Hot, melted rock below the Earth's surface

mantle Thick layer of hot rock between the Earth's crust and core

mud pot Pool of boiling mud in a volcanic region

oceanic crust Outer layer of the Earth with ocean above it

plate boundary Where two or more tectonic plates meet

plug Mass of lava that has hardened and blocked the vent of a volcano

pumice Lightweight form of dried lava that is full of air bubbles

pyroclastic flow Eruption of hot gas, ash, pumice, and rocks that moves rapidly down a volcano's slopes

Ring of Fire Area around the edges of the Pacific Ocean that includes 75 per cent of the world's active volcanoes

shield Type of volcano with gently sloping sides and a shape like an ancient warrior's shield

stalactite Piece of rock that hangs down from the roof of a cave and looks like an icicle

stalagmite Pointed piece of rock slowly growing out of the floor of a cave

stratovolcano Large, steep-sided volcano made of many layers of lava and ash

submarine volcano Volcano that is completely covered by the sea

A **tiltmeter** measures small changes in the slope of the land.

supervolcano Volcano that could have an eruption a thousand times greater than most other volcanoes

tectonic plate Large, slow-moving piece of the Earth's crust

tiltmeter Instrument that measures changes in the slope, or tilt, of the ground. It is used to predict volcanic eruptions

transform boundary Where tectonic plates are sliding past each other

tsunami Giant sea wave created by an earthquake or a volcanic eruption

vent Opening in the Earth's crust out of which lava, ash, rock, and gas erupt

volcano Opening in the Earth's crust, usually in the shape of a mountain, out of which magma, ash, rock, and gas erupt, sometimes explosively

volcanologist Scientist who studies volcanoes

Index

Acknowledgements

DORLING KINDERSLEY would like to thank: Kathleen Teece for editorial assistance, Alexandra Beeden for proofreading, and Helen Peters for the index. The publishers would also like to thank Dr Gill Jolly for the "Meet the expert" interview, Mark Buckley for his geology expertise, and Dan Crisp for his illustrations.

The publisher would like to thank the following for their kind permission to reproduce their photographs:

(Key: a-above; b-below/bottom; c-centre; f-far; l-left; r-right; t-top)

2 Alamy Images: A & J Visage (bl). Corbis: Frans Lanting (bc). 2-3 Alamy Images: Michele Falzone (b). 3 Alamy Images: Tom Pfeiffer (cb). Dorling Kindersley: Natural History Museum, London (fcr, fcrb, crb, crb/gemstone, cr). Dreamstime.com: Odua (bc). 4 NASA: (cl). 4-5 Dorling Kindersley: Dan Crisp. 8 Alamy Images: Tom Bean (bl); Martin Strmiska (tr). 11 Alamy Images: Accent Alaska.com (clb); Brian Overcast (tl); Douglas Peebles Photography (bl); Marek Zuk (tr); Dave Stamboulis (br). Corbis: Michele Falzone / JAI (crb). Dreamstime.com: Craig Hanson / Rssfhs (cra); Lex Schmidt / Lexschmidt (cla). 12 Alamy Images: Nature Picture Library (cl); Robertharding (cr). Corbis: Rolf Schulten / imageBROKER (cla). Dreamstime.com: Alfonsodetomas (cra). 13 Alamy Images: CVI Textures. 14 Alamy Images: Mauricio Alvadorado / COLPRENSA / Xinhua (cla). Getty Images: Archive Farms / Contributor. NASA: (bl). 15 Alamy Images: Tom Pfeiffer (t). Corbis: (b). 16 Alamy Images: Dennis Hallinan. 17 Alamy Images: USGS (t). Rex Shutterstock: KPA / Zuma / REX (br). 20 Alamy Images: Leonid Plotkin (cra); Richard Roscoe / Stocktrek Images (br). Dorling Kindersley: Eden Camp Museum, Yorkshire (bc). Dreamstime.com: Tibinko (bl). 21 Alamy Images: Aflo Co., Ltd (tl); Richard Roscoe / Stocktrek Images (tr); Jeff Smith (bl); David Cole (br). 22-23 Dorling Kindersley: Dan Crisp (Vulcan, Pele, Surtr, Fuchi). 23 Alamy Images: Andrei Nekrassov (br). Corbis: Paul Souders (bc). 24-25 Dorling Kindersley: Dan Crisp. 26-27 Corbis: Thierry Orban / Sygma (c). 26 Corbis: Louise Gubb (bc). 27 Corbis: Peter Turnley (bl). 28-29 Dreamstime.com: Klikk. 29 NASA: Jeff Schmaltz / MODIS Rapid Response Team (cra). 30 Alamy Images: Dennis Frates (cl). 31 Alamy Images: Dinodia Photos (cl). Corbis: Serguei Fomine / Global Look (br); Sergey Krasovskiy / Stocktrek Images (cra). Dreamstime.com: Odua (fcl). 33 Corbis: Christophe Boisvieux (bl); Frans Lanting (ca). 34 Alamy Images: Imagebroker (clb). Photoshot: Xinhua (br). 35 Alamy Images: Imagebroker (cl); Lilyana Vynogradova (cr). Corbis: YNA / epa (bc). 36 Alamy Images: Michele Falzone (cl). Fotolia: Yong Hian Lim (br). 37 Dorling Kindersley: Natural History Museum, London (tr/4 uses, tr/5 uses). Dreamstime.com: Samotrebizan (bl). 38 Alamy Images: epa European Pressphoto Agency creative account (bl). 39 Alamy Images: Olga Kolos (br); A & J Visage (bl). Dorling Kindersley: Dan Crisp (tr). 40-41 Corbis: Marco Restivo / Demotix. 42 Science Photo Library: Jeremy Bishop. 43 Alamy Images: NG Images (crb). 44 Dreamstime.com: Ronald Van Der Beek / Uzuri (c). U.S. Geological Survey: (cl, br). 45 Dorling Kindersley: Dan Crisp (br). U.S. Geological Survey: (br). 46 Corbis: Fadil Aziz / Alcibbum Photograph / Alcibbum Photography (cr). NASA: GSFC / MITI / ERSDAC / JAROS, and the U.S. / Japan ASTER Science Team (br). 47 Alamy Images: Cultura RM (tc); Brian Scantlebury (cb). Corbis: Christian Heinrich / Imagebroker (cl); Valentin Weinhäupl / Westend61 (bl). 48 Dorling Kindersley: Dan Crisp (all 3 illustrations). 50 Getty Images: Eric Vandeville / Contributor (c). 51 Alamy Images: Manfred Gottschalk (c). 52-53 Corbis: Lothar Slabon / Epa. 52 NASA: Earth Observatory image by Jesse Allen, using Landsat data from the U.S. Geological Survey (cl); Earth Observatory image by Jesse Allen, using Landsat data from the U.S. Geological Survey. Caption by Kathryn Hansen (clb). 53 Alamy Images: Arctic Images (br); Andrew Walmsley (cb). Dorling Kindersley: Robert Royse (fcrb). 54 Alamy Images: AF archive (tr); Jeff Rotman (cla). naturepl.com: David Shale (bc). 55 Corbis: Ralph White (bc). Science Photo Library: Philippe Crassous (bl). 56 NASA: (cra, fcra); JPL / Northwestern University (cl); JPL-Caltech (cla); JPL (c, cla); Venus (57 NASA: (c); JPL / USGS (cl); JPL-Caltech / Lunar & Planetary Institute (cr); NASANewHorizons (t). 58 Dorling Kindersley: Dan Crisp (c). 59 Alamy Images: Greg Vaughn (cra). Corbis: Ed Darack / Science Faction (bl). NASA: Jacques Descloitres, MODIS Land Rapid Response Team at NASA GSFC (br). 60 Dorling Kindersley: Dan Crisp (tl, bl). 61 U.S. Geological Survey: (tr)

Cover images: Front: Dorling Kindersley: Dan Crisp cra, Eden Camp Museum, Yorkshire fcra, Natural History Museum, London cr, fcr; Back: Dorling Kindersley: Natural History Museum, London clb; Spine: Dorling Kindersley: Natural History Museum, London; Front Flap: Alamy Images: epa European Pressphoto Agency creative account cl/(front), Olga Kolos tc/(front), tc/(front), A & J Visage cr/(back); Corbis: Lothar Slabon / Epa br/(front); Dorling Kindersley: Robert Royse tr/(back); Dreamstime.com: Oriontrail clb/(front); Fotolia: Yong Hian Lim br/(back); Back Flap: Dorling Kindersley: Gary Ombler / The University of Aberdeen cl; NASA: JSC cb; Back Endpapers: Dorling Kindersley: Museo Archeologico Nazionale di Napoli 0 (Pompeii), Natural History Museum, London 0 (Pocket watch), 0 (Volcanic ash); Fotolia: Pekka Jaakkola / Luminis 0 (Aeroplane); Rex by Shutterstock: Universal History Archive\UIG (Mt. St. Helens)

All other images © Dorling Kindersley
For further information see:
www.dkimages.com

My Findout facts:

Timeline of eruptions

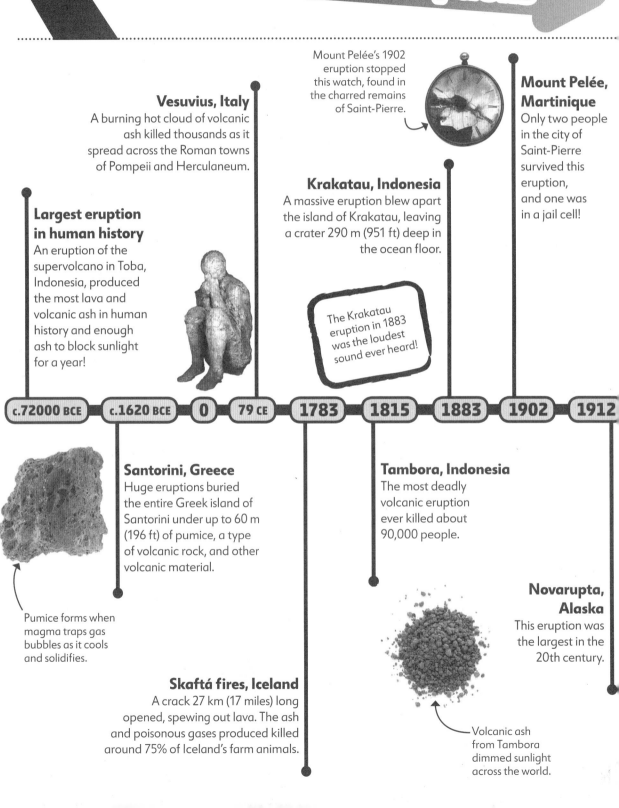

Vesuvius, Italy
A burning hot cloud of volcanic ash killed thousands as it spread across the Roman towns of Pompeii and Herculaneum.

Mount Pelée's 1902 eruption stopped this watch, found in the charred remains of Saint-Pierre.

Mount Pelée, Martinique
Only two people in the city of Saint-Pierre survived this eruption, and one was in a jail cell!

Largest eruption in human history
An eruption of the supervolcano in Toba, Indonesia, produced the most lava and volcanic ash in human history and enough ash to block sunlight for a year!

Krakatau, Indonesia
A massive eruption blew apart the island of Krakatau, leaving a crater 290 m (951 ft) deep in the ocean floor.

The Krakatau eruption in 1883 was the loudest sound ever heard!

c.72000 BCE | c.1620 BCE | 0 | 79 CE | 1783 | 1815 | 1883 | 1902 | 1912

Santorini, Greece
Huge eruptions buried the entire Greek island of Santorini under up to 60 m (196 ft) of pumice, a type of volcanic rock, and other volcanic material.

Tambora, Indonesia
The most deadly volcanic eruption ever killed about 90,000 people.

Pumice forms when magma traps gas bubbles as it cools and solidifies.

Novarupta, Alaska
This eruption was the largest in the 20th century.

Skaftá fires, Iceland
A crack 27 km (17 miles) long opened, spewing out lava. The ash and poisonous gases produced killed around 75% of Iceland's farm animals.

Volcanic ash from Tambora dimmed sunlight across the world.